MEAL PLANNER

Breakfast

Servings	Calories

Snack

Servings	Calories

Lunch

Servings	Calories

Snack

Servings	Calories

Dinner

Servings	Calories

Snack

Servings	Calories

Fitness Activity	Duration	Calories

----------Notes----------

Breakfast

Servings	Calories

Snack

Servings	Calories

Lunch

Servings	Calories

Snack

Servings	Calories

Dinner

Servings	Calories

Snack

Servings	Calories

Fitness Activity	Duration	Calories

Notes

Breakfast	
Servings	Calories

Snack	
Servings	Calories

Lunch	
Servings	Calories

Snack	
Servings	Calories

Dinner	
Servings	Calories

Snack	
Servings	Calories

Fitness Activity	Duration	Calories

-----Notes-----

Breakfast

Servings	Calories

Snack

Servings	Calories

Lunch

Servings	Calories

Snack

Servings	Calories

Dinner

Servings	Calories

Snack

Servings	Calories

Fitness Activity	Duration	Calories

Notes

Breakfast

Servings	Calories

Snack

Servings	Calories

Lunch

Servings	Calories

Snack

Servings	Calories

Dinner

Servings	Calories

Snack

Servings	Calories

Fitness Activity	Duration	Calories

Notes

Breakfast

Servings	Calories

Snack

Servings	Calories

Lunch

Servings	Calories

Snack

Servings	Calories

Dinner

Servings	Calories

Snack

Servings	Calories

Fitness Activity	Duration	Calories

Notes

Breakfast

Servings	Calories

Snack

Servings	Calories

Lunch

Servings	Calories

Snack

Servings	Calories

Dinner

Servings	Calories

Snack

Servings	Calories

Fitness Activity	Duration	Calories

-------------------------Notes-------------------------

Breakfast

Servings	Calories

Snack

Servings	Calories

Lunch

Servings	Calories

Snack

Servings	Calories

Dinner

Servings	Calories

Snack

Servings	Calories

Fitness Activity	Duration	Calories

Notes

Breakfast

Servings	Calories

Snack

Servings	Calories

Lunch

Servings	Calories

Snack

Servings	Calories

Dinner

Servings	Calories

Snack

Servings	Calories

Fitness Activity	Duration	Calories

Notes

Breakfast

Servings	Calories

Snack

Servings	Calories

Lunch

Servings	Calories

Snack

Servings	Calories

Dinner

Servings	Calories

Snack

Servings	Calories

Fitness Activity	Duration	Calories

Notes

Breakfast

Servings	Calories

Snack

Servings	Calories

Lunch

Servings	Calories

Snack

Servings	Calories

Dinner

Servings	Calories

Snack

Servings	Calories

Fitness Activity	Duration	Calories

Notes

Breakfast

Servings	Calories

Snack

Servings	Calories

Lunch

Servings	Calories

Snack

Servings	Calories

Dinner

Servings	Calories

Snack

Servings	Calories

Fitness Activity	Duration	Calories

Notes

Breakfast

Servings	Calories

Snack

Servings	Calories

Lunch

Servings	Calories

Snack

Servings	Calories

Dinner

Servings	Calories

Snack

Servings	Calories

Fitness Activity	Duration	Calories

Notes

Breakfast

Servings	Calories

Snack

Servings	Calories

Lunch

Servings	Calories

Snack

Servings	Calories

Dinner

Servings	Calories

Snack

Servings	Calories

Fitness Activity	Duration	Calories

Notes

Breakfast

Servings	Calories

Snack

Servings	Calories

Lunch

Servings	Calories

Snack

Servings	Calories

Dinner

Servings	Calories

Snack

Servings	Calories

Fitness Activity	Duration	Calories

-------------------------------Notes-------------------------------

Breakfast

Servings	Calories

Snack

Servings	Calories

Lunch

Servings	Calories

Snack

Servings	Calories

Dinner

Servings	Calories

Snack

Servings	Calories

Fitness Activity	Duration	Calories

Notes

Breakfast

Servings	Calories

Snack

Servings	Calories

Lunch

Servings	Calories

Snack

Servings	Calories

Dinner

Servings	Calories

Snack

Servings	Calories

Fitness Activity	Duration	Calories

Notes

Breakfast

Servings	Calories

Snack

Servings	Calories

Lunch

Servings	Calories

Snack

Servings	Calories

Dinner

Servings	Calories

Snack

Servings	Calories

Fitness Activity	Duration	Calories

Notes

Breakfast

Servings	Calories

Snack

Servings	Calories

Lunch

Servings	Calories

Snack

Servings	Calories

Dinner

Servings	Calories

Snack

Servings	Calories

Fitness Activity	Duration	Calories

-----------------------------Notes-----------------------------

Breakfast

Servings	Calories

Snack

Servings	Calories

Lunch

Servings	Calories

Snack

Servings	Calories

Dinner

Servings	Calories

Snack

Servings	Calories

Fitness Activity	Duration	Calories

Notes

Breakfast

Servings	Calories

Snack

Servings	Calories

Lunch

Servings	Calories

Snack

Servings	Calories

Dinner

Servings	Calories

Snack

Servings	Calories

Fitness Activity	Duration	Calories

Notes

<table>
<tr><td colspan="2"><h2>Breakfast</h2></td><td colspan="2"><h2>Snack</h2></td></tr>
<tr><td>Servings</td><td>Calories</td><td>Servings</td><td>Calories</td></tr>
<tr><td></td><td></td><td></td><td></td></tr>
<tr><td></td><td></td><td></td><td></td></tr>
<tr><td></td><td></td><td></td><td></td></tr>
<tr><td></td><td></td><td></td><td></td></tr>
</table>

Lunch

Snack

Servings	Calories	Servings	Calories

Dinner

Snack

Servings	Calories	Servings	Calories

Fitness Activity	Duration	Calories

Notes

Breakfast

Servings	Calories

Snack

Servings	Calories

Lunch

Servings	Calories

Snack

Servings	Calories

Dinner

Servings	Calories

Snack

Servings	Calories

Fitness Activity	Duration	Calories

-----------------------Notes-----------------------

Breakfast

Servings	Calories

Snack

Servings	Calories

Lunch

Servings	Calories

Snack

Servings	Calories

Dinner

Servings	Calories

Snack

Servings	Calories

Fitness Activity	Duration	Calories

Notes

Breakfast

Servings	Calories

Snack

Servings	Calories

Lunch

Servings	Calories

Snack

Servings	Calories

Dinner

Servings	Calories

Snack

Servings	Calories

Fitness Activity	Duration	Calories

Notes

Breakfast

Servings	Calories

Snack

Servings	Calories

Lunch

Servings	Calories

Snack

Servings	Calories

Dinner

Servings	Calories

Snack

Servings	Calories

Fitness Activity	Duration	Calories

-------------------------------Notes-------------------------------

Breakfast

Servings	Calories

Snack

Servings	Calories

Lunch

Servings	Calories

Snack

Servings	Calories

Dinner

Servings	Calories

Snack

Servings	Calories

Fitness Activity	Duration	Calories

-------------------------------Notes-------------------------------

Breakfast

Servings	Calories

Snack

Servings	Calories

Lunch

Servings	Calories

Snack

Servings	Calories

Dinner

Servings	Calories

Snack

Servings	Calories

Fitness Activity	Duration	Calories

Notes

Breakfast

Servings	Calories

Snack

Servings	Calories

Lunch

Servings	Calories

Snack

Servings	Calories

Dinner

Servings	Calories

Snack

Servings	Calories

Fitness Activity	Duration	Calories

Notes

Breakfast

Servings	Calories

Snack

Servings	Calories

Lunch

Servings	Calories

Snack

Servings	Calories

Dinner

Servings	Calories

Snack

Servings	Calories

Fitness Activity	Duration	Calories

Notes

Breakfast

Servings	Calories

Snack

Servings	Calories

Lunch

Servings	Calories

Snack

Servings	Calories

Dinner

Servings	Calories

Snack

Servings	Calories

Fitness Activity	Duration	Calories

Notes

Breakfast

Servings	Calories

Snack

Servings	Calories

Lunch

Servings	Calories

Snack

Servings	Calories

Dinner

Servings	Calories

Snack

Servings	Calories

Fitness Activity	Duration	Calories

Notes

Breakfast

Servings	Calories

Snack

Servings	Calories

Lunch

Servings	Calories

Snack

Servings	Calories

Dinner

Servings	Calories

Snack

Servings	Calories

Fitness Activity	Duration	Calories

Notes

Breakfast

Servings	Calories

Snack

Servings	Calories

Lunch

Servings	Calories

Snack

Servings	Calories

Dinner

Servings	Calories

Snack

Servings	Calories

Fitness Activity	Duration	Calories

Notes

Breakfast

Servings	Calories

Snack

Servings	Calories

Lunch

Servings	Calories

Snack

Servings	Calories

Dinner

Servings	Calories

Snack

Servings	Calories

Fitness Activity	Duration	Calories

Notes

Breakfast

Servings	Calories

Snack

Servings	Calories

Lunch

Servings	Calories

Snack

Servings	Calories

Dinner

Servings	Calories

Snack

Servings	Calories

Fitness Activity	Duration	Calories

Notes

Breakfast

Servings	Calories

Snack

Servings	Calories

Lunch

Servings	Calories

Snack

Servings	Calories

Dinner

Servings	Calories

Snack

Servings	Calories

Fitness Activity	Duration	Calories

Notes

Breakfast

Servings	Calories

Snack

Servings	Calories

Lunch

Servings	Calories

Snack

Servings	Calories

Dinner

Servings	Calories

Snack

Servings	Calories

Fitness Activity	Duration	Calories

Notes

Breakfast	
Servings	Calories

Snack	
Servings	Calories

Lunch	
Servings	Calories

Snack	
Servings	Calories

Dinner	
Servings	Calories

Snack	
Servings	Calories

Fitness Activity	Duration	Calories

-------------------------Notes-------------------------

Breakfast

Servings	Calories

Snack

Servings	Calories

Lunch

Servings	Calories

Snack

Servings	Calories

Dinner

Servings	Calories

Snack

Servings	Calories

Fitness Activity	Duration	Calories

Notes

Breakfast	
Servings	Calories

Snack	
Servings	Calories

Lunch	
Servings	Calories

Snack	
Servings	Calories

Dinner	
Servings	Calories

Snack	
Servings	Calories

Fitness Activity	Duration	Calories

Notes

Breakfast

Servings	Calories

Snack

Servings	Calories

Lunch

Servings	Calories

Snack

Servings	Calories

Dinner

Servings	Calories

Snack

Servings	Calories

Fitness Activity	Duration	Calories

Notes

Breakfast

Servings	Calories

Snack

Servings	Calories

Lunch

Servings	Calories

Snack

Servings	Calories

Dinner

Servings	Calories

Snack

Servings	Calories

Fitness Activity	Duration	Calories

-------------------------Notes-------------------------

Breakfast

Servings	Calories

Snack

Servings	Calories

Lunch

Servings	Calories

Snack

Servings	Calories

Dinner

Servings	Calories

Snack

Servings	Calories

Fitness Activity	Duration	Calories

-------------------------------Notes-------------------------------

Breakfast

Servings	Calories

Snack

Servings	Calories

Lunch

Servings	Calories

Snack

Servings	Calories

Dinner

Servings	Calories

Snack

Servings	Calories

Fitness Activity	Duration	Calories

Notes

Breakfast

Servings	Calories

Snack

Servings	Calories

Lunch

Servings	Calories

Snack

Servings	Calories

Dinner

Servings	Calories

Snack

Servings	Calories

Fitness Activity	Duration	Calories

Notes

Breakfast

Servings	Calories

Snack

Servings	Calories

Lunch

Servings	Calories

Snack

Servings	Calories

Dinner

Servings	Calories

Snack

Servings	Calories

Fitness Activity	Duration	Calories

Notes

Breakfast

Servings	Calories

Snack

Servings	Calories

Lunch

Servings	Calories

Snack

Servings	Calories

Dinner

Servings	Calories

Snack

Servings	Calories

Fitness Activity	Duration	Calories

Notes

Breakfast

Servings	Calories

Snack

Servings	Calories

Lunch

Servings	Calories

Snack

Servings	Calories

Dinner

Servings	Calories

Snack

Servings	Calories

Fitness Activity	Duration	Calories

Notes

Breakfast

Servings	Calories

Snack

Servings	Calories

Lunch

Servings	Calories

Snack

Servings	Calories

Dinner

Servings	Calories

Snack

Servings	Calories

Fitness Activity	Duration	Calories

-------------------------Notes-------------------------

Breakfast

Servings	Calories

Snack

Servings	Calories

Lunch

Servings	Calories

Snack

Servings	Calories

Dinner

Servings	Calories

Snack

Servings	Calories

Fitness Activity	Duration	Calories

-------------------------Notes-------------------------

Breakfast	
Servings	Calories

Snack	
Servings	Calories

Lunch	
Servings	Calories

Snack	
Servings	Calories

Dinner	
Servings	Calories

Snack	
Servings	Calories

Fitness Activity	Duration	Calories

Notes

Breakfast	
Servings	Calories

Snack	
Servings	Calories

Lunch	
Servings	Calories

Snack	
Servings	Calories

Dinner	
Servings	Calories

Snack	
Servings	Calories

Fitness Activity	Duration	Calories

Notes

Breakfast

Servings	Calories

Snack

Servings	Calories

Lunch

Servings	Calories

Snack

Servings	Calories

Dinner

Servings	Calories

Snack

Servings	Calories

Fitness Activity	Duration	Calories

Notes

Breakfast	
Servings	Calories

Snack	
Servings	Calories

Lunch	
Servings	Calories

Snack	
Servings	Calories

Dinner	
Servings	Calories

Snack	
Servings	Calories

Fitness Activity	Duration	Calories

Notes

<table>
<tr><th colspan="2">Breakfast</th><th colspan="2">Snack</th></tr>
<tr><td>Servings</td><td>Calories</td><td>Servings</td><td>Calories</td></tr>
<tr><td></td><td></td><td></td><td></td></tr>
<tr><td></td><td></td><td></td><td></td></tr>
<tr><td></td><td></td><td></td><td></td></tr>
<tr><td></td><td></td><td></td><td></td></tr>
</table>

<table>
<tr><th colspan="2">Lunch</th><th colspan="2">Snack</th></tr>
<tr><td>Servings</td><td>Calories</td><td>Servings</td><td>Calories</td></tr>
<tr><td></td><td></td><td></td><td></td></tr>
<tr><td></td><td></td><td></td><td></td></tr>
<tr><td></td><td></td><td></td><td></td></tr>
<tr><td></td><td></td><td></td><td></td></tr>
</table>

<table>
<tr><th colspan="2">Dinner</th><th colspan="2">Snack</th></tr>
<tr><td>Servings</td><td>Calories</td><td>Servings</td><td>Calories</td></tr>
<tr><td></td><td></td><td></td><td></td></tr>
<tr><td></td><td></td><td></td><td></td></tr>
<tr><td></td><td></td><td></td><td></td></tr>
<tr><td></td><td></td><td></td><td></td></tr>
</table>

Fitness Activity	Duration	Calories

Notes

Breakfast

Servings	Calories

Snack

Servings	Calories

Lunch

Servings	Calories

Snack

Servings	Calories

Dinner

Servings	Calories

Snack

Servings	Calories

Fitness Activity	Duration	Calories

Notes

<table>
<tr><th colspan="2">Breakfast</th><th colspan="2">Snack</th></tr>
<tr><td>Servings</td><td>Calories</td><td>Servings</td><td>Calories</td></tr>
<tr><td></td><td></td><td></td><td></td></tr>
<tr><td></td><td></td><td></td><td></td></tr>
<tr><td></td><td></td><td></td><td></td></tr>
<tr><td></td><td></td><td></td><td></td></tr>
</table>

<table>
<tr><th colspan="2">Lunch</th><th colspan="2">Snack</th></tr>
<tr><td>Servings</td><td>Calories</td><td>Servings</td><td>Calories</td></tr>
<tr><td></td><td></td><td></td><td></td></tr>
<tr><td></td><td></td><td></td><td></td></tr>
<tr><td></td><td></td><td></td><td></td></tr>
<tr><td></td><td></td><td></td><td></td></tr>
</table>

<table>
<tr><th colspan="2">Dinner</th><th colspan="2">Snack</th></tr>
<tr><td>Servings</td><td>Calories</td><td>Servings</td><td>Calories</td></tr>
<tr><td></td><td></td><td></td><td></td></tr>
<tr><td></td><td></td><td></td><td></td></tr>
<tr><td></td><td></td><td></td><td></td></tr>
<tr><td></td><td></td><td></td><td></td></tr>
</table>

Fitness Activity	Duration	Calories

Notes

Breakfast

Servings	Calories

Snack

Servings	Calories

Lunch

Servings	Calories

Snack

Servings	Calories

Dinner

Servings	Calories

Snack

Servings	Calories

Fitness Activity	Duration	Calories

Notes

Breakfast

Servings	Calories

Snack

Servings	Calories

Lunch

Servings	Calories

Snack

Servings	Calories

Dinner

Servings	Calories

Snack

Servings	Calories

Fitness Activity	Duration	Calories

Notes

Breakfast

Servings	Calories

Snack

Servings	Calories

Lunch

Servings	Calories

Snack

Servings	Calories

Dinner

Servings	Calories

Snack

Servings	Calories

Fitness Activity	Duration	Calories

Notes

Breakfast

Servings	Calories

Snack

Servings	Calories

Lunch

Servings	Calories

Snack

Servings	Calories

Dinner

Servings	Calories

Snack

Servings	Calories

Fitness Activity	Duration	Calories

Notes

Breakfast

Servings	Calories

Snack

Servings	Calories

Lunch

Servings	Calories

Snack

Servings	Calories

Dinner

Servings	Calories

Snack

Servings	Calories

Fitness Activity	Duration	Calories

Notes

Breakfast

Servings	Calories

Snack

Servings	Calories

Lunch

Servings	Calories

Snack

Servings	Calories

Dinner

Servings	Calories

Snack

Servings	Calories

Fitness Activity	Duration	Calories

Notes

Breakfast

Servings	Calories

Snack

Servings	Calories

Lunch

Servings	Calories

Snack

Servings	Calories

Dinner

Servings	Calories

Snack

Servings	Calories

Fitness Activity	Duration	Calories

Notes

Breakfast

Servings	Calories

Snack

Servings	Calories

Lunch

Servings	Calories

Snack

Servings	Calories

Dinner

Servings	Calories

Snack

Servings	Calories

Fitness Activity	Duration	Calories

Notes

Breakfast

Servings	Calories

Snack

Servings	Calories

Lunch

Servings	Calories

Snack

Servings	Calories

Dinner

Servings	Calories

Snack

Servings	Calories

Fitness Activity	Duration	Calories

Notes

Breakfast

Servings	Calories

Snack

Servings	Calories

Lunch

Servings	Calories

Snack

Servings	Calories

Dinner

Servings	Calories

Snack

Servings	Calories

Fitness Activity	Duration	Calories

Notes

Breakfast

Servings	Calories

Snack

Servings	Calories

Lunch

Servings	Calories

Snack

Servings	Calories

Dinner

Servings	Calories

Snack

Servings	Calories

Fitness Activity	Duration	Calories

Notes

Breakfast

Servings	Calories

Snack

Servings	Calories

Lunch

Servings	Calories

Snack

Servings	Calories

Dinner

Servings	Calories

Snack

Servings	Calories

Fitness Activity	Duration	Calories

Notes

Breakfast

Servings	Calories

Snack

Servings	Calories

Lunch

Servings	Calories

Snack

Servings	Calories

Dinner

Servings	Calories

Snack

Servings	Calories

Fitness Activity	Duration	Calories

Notes

Breakfast

Servings	Calories

Snack

Servings	Calories

Lunch

Servings	Calories

Snack

Servings	Calories

Dinner

Servings	Calories

Snack

Servings	Calories

Fitness Activity	Duration	Calories

Notes

Breakfast

Servings	Calories

Snack

Servings	Calories

Lunch

Servings	Calories

Snack

Servings	Calories

Dinner

Servings	Calories

Snack

Servings	Calories

Fitness Activity	Duration	Calories

-----Notes-----

Breakfast

Servings	Calories

Snack

Servings	Calories

Lunch

Servings	Calories

Snack

Servings	Calories

Dinner

Servings	Calories

Snack

Servings	Calories

Fitness Activity	Duration	Calories

Notes

Breakfast

Servings	Calories

Snack

Servings	Calories

Lunch

Servings	Calories

Snack

Servings	Calories

Dinner

Servings	Calories

Snack

Servings	Calories

Fitness Activity	Duration	Calories

Notes

Breakfast

Servings	Calories

Snack

Servings	Calories

Lunch

Servings	Calories

Snack

Servings	Calories

Dinner

Servings	Calories

Snack

Servings	Calories

Fitness Activity	Duration	Calories

Notes

Breakfast

Servings	Calories

Snack

Servings	Calories

Lunch

Servings	Calories

Snack

Servings	Calories

Dinner

Servings	Calories

Snack

Servings	Calories

Fitness Activity	Duration	Calories

Notes

Breakfast

Servings	Calories

Snack

Servings	Calories

Lunch

Servings	Calories

Snack

Servings	Calories

Dinner

Servings	Calories

Snack

Servings	Calories

Fitness Activity	Duration	Calories

Notes

Breakfast

Servings	Calories

Snack

Servings	Calories

Lunch

Servings	Calories

Snack

Servings	Calories

Dinner

Servings	Calories

Snack

Servings	Calories

Fitness Activity	Duration	Calories

Notes

Breakfast

Servings	Calories

Snack

Servings	Calories

Lunch

Servings	Calories

Snack

Servings	Calories

Dinner

Servings	Calories

Snack

Servings	Calories

Fitness Activity	Duration	Calories

Notes

Breakfast

Servings	Calories

Snack

Servings	Calories

Lunch

Servings	Calories

Snack

Servings	Calories

Dinner

Servings	Calories

Snack

Servings	Calories

Fitness Activity	Duration	Calories

Notes

Breakfast

Servings	Calories

Snack

Servings	Calories

Lunch

Servings	Calories

Snack

Servings	Calories

Dinner

Servings	Calories

Snack

Servings	Calories

Fitness Activity	Duration	Calories

Notes

Breakfast

Servings	Calories

Snack

Servings	Calories

Lunch

Servings	Calories

Snack

Servings	Calories

Dinner

Servings	Calories

Snack

Servings	Calories

Fitness Activity	Duration	Calories

Notes

Breakfast

Servings	Calories

Snack

Servings	Calories

Lunch

Servings	Calories

Snack

Servings	Calories

Dinner

Servings	Calories

Snack

Servings	Calories

Fitness Activity	Duration	Calories

Notes

Breakfast

Servings	Calories

Snack

Servings	Calories

Lunch

Servings	Calories

Snack

Servings	Calories

Dinner

Servings	Calories

Snack

Servings	Calories

Fitness Activity	Duration	Calories

-----------------------------Notes-----------------------------

Breakfast

Servings	Calories

Snack

Servings	Calories

Lunch

Servings	Calories

Snack

Servings	Calories

Dinner

Servings	Calories

Snack

Servings	Calories

Fitness Activity	Duration	Calories

Notes

Breakfast

Servings	Calories

Snack

Servings	Calories

Lunch

Servings	Calories

Snack

Servings	Calories

Dinner

Servings	Calories

Snack

Servings	Calories

Fitness Activity	Duration	Calories

Notes

Breakfast

Servings	Calories

Snack

Servings	Calories

Lunch

Servings	Calories

Snack

Servings	Calories

Dinner

Servings	Calories

Snack

Servings	Calories

Fitness Activity	Duration	Calories

Notes

Breakfast

Servings	Calories

Snack

Servings	Calories

Lunch

Servings	Calories

Snack

Servings	Calories

Dinner

Servings	Calories

Snack

Servings	Calories

Fitness Activity	Duration	Calories

Notes

Breakfast

Servings	Calories

Snack

Servings	Calories

Lunch

Servings	Calories

Snack

Servings	Calories

Dinner

Servings	Calories

Snack

Servings	Calories

Fitness Activity	Duration	Calories

Notes

Breakfast

Servings	Calories

Snack

Servings	Calories

Lunch

Servings	Calories

Snack

Servings	Calories

Dinner

Servings	Calories

Snack

Servings	Calories

Fitness Activity	Duration	Calories

Notes

Breakfast

Servings	Calories

Snack

Servings	Calories

Lunch

Servings	Calories

Snack

Servings	Calories

Dinner

Servings	Calories

Snack

Servings	Calories

Fitness Activity	Duration	Calories

Notes

Breakfast

Servings	Calories

Snack

Servings	Calories

Lunch

Servings	Calories

Snack

Servings	Calories

Dinner

Servings	Calories

Snack

Servings	Calories

Fitness Activity	Duration	Calories

-----Notes-----

Breakfast

Servings	Calories

Snack

Servings	Calories

Lunch

Servings	Calories

Snack

Servings	Calories

Dinner

Servings	Calories

Snack

Servings	Calories

Fitness Activity	Duration	Calories

Notes

Breakfast

Servings	Calories

Snack

Servings	Calories

Lunch

Servings	Calories

Snack

Servings	Calories

Dinner

Servings	Calories

Snack

Servings	Calories

Fitness Activity	Duration	Calories

Notes

Breakfast

Servings	Calories

Snack

Servings	Calories

Lunch

Servings	Calories

Snack

Servings	Calories

Dinner

Servings	Calories

Snack

Servings	Calories

Fitness Activity	Duration	Calories

Notes

Breakfast

Servings	Calories

Snack

Servings	Calories

Lunch

Servings	Calories

Snack

Servings	Calories

Dinner

Servings	Calories

Snack

Servings	Calories

Fitness Activity	Duration	Calories

Notes

Breakfast

Servings	Calories

Snack

Servings	Calories

Lunch

Servings	Calories

Snack

Servings	Calories

Dinner

Servings	Calories

Snack

Servings	Calories

Fitness Activity	Duration	Calories

Notes

Breakfast

Servings	Calories

Snack

Servings	Calories

Lunch

Servings	Calories

Snack

Servings	Calories

Dinner

Servings	Calories

Snack

Servings	Calories

Fitness Activity	Duration	Calories

Notes

Breakfast

Servings	Calories

Snack

Servings	Calories

Lunch

Servings	Calories

Snack

Servings	Calories

Dinner

Servings	Calories

Snack

Servings	Calories

Fitness Activity	Duration	Calories

Notes

Breakfast

Servings	Calories

Snack

Servings	Calories

Lunch

Servings	Calories

Snack

Servings	Calories

Dinner

Servings	Calories

Snack

Servings	Calories

Fitness Activity	Duration	Calories

Notes

Breakfast

Servings	Calories

Snack

Servings	Calories

Lunch

Servings	Calories

Snack

Servings	Calories

Dinner

Servings	Calories

Snack

Servings	Calories

Fitness Activity	Duration	Calories

Notes

Breakfast

Servings	Calories

Snack

Servings	Calories

Lunch

Servings	Calories

Snack

Servings	Calories

Dinner

Servings	Calories

Snack

Servings	Calories

Fitness Activity	Duration	Calories

Notes

Breakfast

Servings	Calories

Snack

Servings	Calories

Lunch

Servings	Calories

Snack

Servings	Calories

Dinner

Servings	Calories

Snack

Servings	Calories

Fitness Activity	Duration	Calories

Notes

Breakfast

Servings	Calories

Snack

Servings	Calories

Lunch

Servings	Calories

Snack

Servings	Calories

Dinner

Servings	Calories

Snack

Servings	Calories

Fitness Activity	Duration	Calories

Notes

Breakfast

Servings	Calories

Snack

Servings	Calories

Lunch

Servings	Calories

Snack

Servings	Calories

Dinner

Servings	Calories

Snack

Servings	Calories

Fitness Activity	Duration	Calories

Notes

Breakfast

Servings	Calories

Snack

Servings	Calories

Lunch

Servings	Calories

Snack

Servings	Calories

Dinner

Servings	Calories

Snack

Servings	Calories

Fitness Activity	Duration	Calories

Notes

Breakfast

Servings	Calories

Snack

Servings	Calories

Lunch

Servings	Calories

Snack

Servings	Calories

Dinner

Servings	Calories

Snack

Servings	Calories

Fitness Activity	Duration	Calories

Notes

Breakfast

Servings	Calories

Snack

Servings	Calories

Lunch

Servings	Calories

Snack

Servings	Calories

Dinner

Servings	Calories

Snack

Servings	Calories

Fitness Activity	Duration	Calories

Notes

Breakfast

Servings	Calories

Snack

Servings	Calories

Lunch

Servings	Calories

Snack

Servings	Calories

Dinner

Servings	Calories

Snack

Servings	Calories

Fitness Activity	Duration	Calories

Notes

Breakfast

Servings	Calories

Snack

Servings	Calories

Lunch

Servings	Calories

Snack

Servings	Calories

Dinner

Servings	Calories

Snack

Servings	Calories

Fitness Activity	Duration	Calories

Notes

Breakfast

Servings	Calories

Snack

Servings	Calories

Lunch

Servings	Calories

Snack

Servings	Calories

Dinner

Servings	Calories

Snack

Servings	Calories

Fitness Activity	Duration	Calories

Notes

Breakfast

Servings	Calories

Snack

Servings	Calories

Lunch

Servings	Calories

Snack

Servings	Calories

Dinner

Servings	Calories

Snack

Servings	Calories

Fitness Activity	Duration	Calories

Notes

Breakfast

Servings	Calories

Snack

Servings	Calories

Lunch

Servings	Calories

Snack

Servings	Calories

Dinner

Servings	Calories

Snack

Servings	Calories

Fitness Activity	Duration	Calories

Notes

Breakfast

Servings	Calories

Snack

Servings	Calories

Lunch

Servings	Calories

Snack

Servings	Calories

Dinner

Servings	Calories

Snack

Servings	Calories

Fitness Activity	Duration	Calories

---Notes---

Breakfast

Servings	Calories

Snack

Servings	Calories

Lunch

Servings	Calories

Snack

Servings	Calories

Dinner

Servings	Calories

Snack

Servings	Calories

Fitness Activity	Duration	Calories

Notes

Breakfast

Servings	Calories

Snack

Servings	Calories

Lunch

Servings	Calories

Snack

Servings	Calories

Dinner

Servings	Calories

Snack

Servings	Calories

Fitness Activity	Duration	Calories

Notes

Breakfast

Servings	Calories

Snack

Servings	Calories

Lunch

Servings	Calories

Snack

Servings	Calories

Dinner

Servings	Calories

Snack

Servings	Calories

Fitness Activity	Duration	Calories

Notes

Breakfast

Servings	Calories

Snack

Servings	Calories

Lunch

Servings	Calories

Snack

Servings	Calories

Dinner

Servings	Calories

Snack

Servings	Calories

Fitness Activity	Duration	Calories

Notes

Breakfast

Servings	Calories

Snack

Servings	Calories

Lunch

Servings	Calories

Snack

Servings	Calories

Dinner

Servings	Calories

Snack

Servings	Calories

Fitness Activity	Duration	Calories

Notes